Echoes of Freedom Past

Reclaiming and Restoring Liberty

Warren Bluhm

2022

ECHOES OF FREEDOM PAST

Reclaiming and Restoring Liberty

© 2022, 2023 Warren Bluhm

Second edition February 2023

Cover image © Anyaberkut | Dreamstime.com

ISBN 979-8-9863331-3-7

Liberty, finally, is not a box into which people are forced. Liberty is a space in which people may live. It does not tell you how they will live. It says, eternally, only that we can.

— Karl Hess

Table of Contents

ECHOES OF FREEDOM PAST

Introduction: Echoes of Freedom Past

In a blink it all changed.

In reality, it took years, perhaps all our lives, but the realization, that happened in a blink.

One moment everyone was pretending like we had always been free, and the next moment everyone was pretending like we had never. It was disorienting for those of us who remembered our previous lives.

"Don't you see how wrong all this is?" we said.

"Stop with the misinformation, you stooge of a foreign government," replied our friends, or those we had counted as friends until everything changed in a blink.

One moment we were united — "They hate our freedoms; if we lose our freedom, then the terrorists have won" — and the next moment, the terrorists had won. We lived in terror — terrified of inflation, sickness, supply-chain issues, neighbors, strangers, Russians, and most of all the opposite political party.

This is a little book about what used to be, what is, and what could be if we wish to reclaim it.

There is a section about freedom and the Bill of Rights.

There is a section about what has been happening in the last several years, and the blink.

And there is a section of hope for the future, because I truly believe most of us want to be free, want to be left alone to live our personal vision of our best life, and want to respect everyone's right to life, liberty, and pursuit of happiness, as long as they don't infringe on other people's equal rights to those things.

The thoughts in this collection, for the most part, originally appeared in my blog, most of them in recent years but some from as long ago as 2008. My blog is not "only" about these themes. Most of the time I write about creativity, pop culture past and present, and try to encourage folks to see the world in a positive light.

INTRODUCTION

Even when I touch on our ridiculous times, I try to do so with a sense of humor and with a confidence that most people want to be free. But occasionally even the most optimistic person has to look at what's happening in our nation and world with a bit of concern if not alarm.

In the end, most days, my optimism wins, because that all-important declaration is still circulating, still reaching hearts, still resonating in souls — you know the one, the declaration that:

"We hold these truths to be self-evident, that all Men are created equal, that they are endowed by their Creator with certain unalienable Rights, that among these are Life, Liberty, and the Pursuit of Happiness ..."

Introduction: Your humble host

Hi there. I'm Warren Bluhm. By day I am editor and one of a handful of reporters for a small family of community newspapers in rural Wisconsin. When away from that task, I have written and published (as of June 2022) four books of fiction and six collections of short essays from my blog, and I have published nine editions of vintage works — some familiar, some not so much — that deserve to be remembered and preserved. I'm not done yet, either.

I produced 80 episodes of a podcast called *Uncle Warren's Attic*, 150 episodes of a podcast called *Ikthuscast*, and 13 episodes of a podcast called *Uncle Warren's 78 Revolutions Per Minute*. My first foray into

INTRODUCTION

podcasting was a serialized reading of my first novel, *The Imaginary Bomb*. I bought a new microphone with plans to podcast again, but years have passed since I did so.

I like old stuff, stuff that's even older than the great stuff that was new when I was a kid, like the Fantastic Four and Spider-Man comic books and the original Star Trek. I have boxes and boxes of 78 rpm records, shelves and shelves of LPs and books, and other relics of olden times. If you made me list my all-time favorite recordings, "Frenesi" by Artie Shaw, "Sing Sing Sing" by Benny Goodman, and "Powerhouse" by Raymond Scott would be on the list, along with beaucoup examples from my actual lifetime.

I like independence and independent stuff. *Ikthuscast* was packed with songs created by Christian musicians who eschewed the gatekeepers and release their work on independent platforms. I publish my work independently rather than slog my way through the traditional process that can take years before a book sees the light of day, if ever. I tend to take stock every year around May 19, the anniversary of my first day as a full-time adult, the day after college graduation, when I assumed total responsibility for feeding myself, lo, these 47 years ago.

After all that time, some days I'm tired, if I'm honest. Most days, though, I remember how much fun it has been to do what I do, and I appreciate my companions along the way, especially the big-hearted woman who shares a house, two golden retrievers and a cat with me. I hope and pray our remaining time is full of love and peace and adventure.

I think about peace and wonder why some folks are hell-bent on killing people and blowing up things. My mother's favorite president, Dwight Eisenhower, said a number of wise things in his farewell address, the wisest being, "we must guard against the acquisition of unwarranted influence, whether sought or unsought, by the military-industrial complex. The potential for the disastrous rise of misplaced power exists and will persist." The extent to which we have let down that guard is discouraging, to be sure.

INTRODUCTION

Still, I can't help but believe, against all odds, that it's going to be all right in the end. Our history is a slow but steady march toward unfurling fists and reaching out our hands in friendship, a meandering walk away from resolving our differences with weapons and toward nonviolent solutions, a growing abhorrence of war and embracing peace. Too many war mongers hold onto their sabers and rattle them into the night as they cling to power, but their numbers are dwindling.

Maybe I'm overly optimistic because it's a sunny spring day and the world outside my window is dominated at last by the color green, after too many cold months of brown and white. Maybe I'm overly content because there's a 10-month-old puppy at my feet, convalescing from her spay surgery of two days ago and healing nicely so far. But I'm optimistic and content, so you'll just have to deal.

Where do we go from here? What happens next? We always have some idea, but there are always surprises. That's what keeps life interesting.

ECHOES OF FREEDOM PAST

Freedom

and the Bill of Rights

ECHOES OF FREEDOM PAST

The cost of freedom

Freedom is, in fact, free. We are born free. Our creator bestows freedom on us upon birth, including the right to life, liberty and the pursuit of happiness. The cost they talk about is the cost of protecting and defending those rights. There is also the cost of assuming the consequences of your free words and actions.

Who are these people who would attack your right to life, liberty and the pursuit of happiness? Well, when the phrase was coined and placed in a certain Declaration, the main culprits were a certain monarch and his minions, a king who was proclaimed the ruler over persons who lived thousands of miles from his throne room. Not surprisingly, those persons squirmed under his thumb and separated themselves from his rule.

As often happens, the ruler's response was to commit violence. Ruling by violence never wins friends, but rulers have never learned this. It's the height of arrogance to presume to rule another individual, as if the ruler knows that person's needs more intimately than the person does. But centuries and millennia have passed, and rulers still rule with threats and violence and anger and hatred.

Every so often a person tries to lead — lead, not rule — without violence but rather with love, without chains but rather with freedom, and along come the rulers to squash them. Still, their names and messages resonate through history long after their critics and killers have passed to dust. These leaders continue to be examples of hope, icons to whom we turn when we dream of a better world.

Rulers inevitably disappoint their subjects. Rulers inevitably harm their subjects. It is not human nature to be ruled or whipped into obedience, but rulers don't understand this and pull out the whips and chains and edicts and orders anyway.

Freedom is often defined as the absence of some external force. Freedom is better defined as the realization that the "force" has no real power and we are free to come and go as we please. Within reason, of course: No one is free to steal from or kill a neighbor, although a ruler might think he can and often does.

Without this realization that we are free, we become slaves of one sort or another. Rulers may exert ownership over our lives and property and persons, but they can never own our selves, that soul that resides in our hearts and heads. All they can do is restrict and, well, govern. But we are still free.

We can still discern right from wrong, freedom from slavery, war from peace, truth from deception, fact from fiction. They hate our freedom, but what the Creator has given, no human can fully remove. It drives them crazy, which is why so many rulers act as if they are simply insane. In fact, they are.

Because they can't take freedom away from us.

Freedom is not for the faint of heart

You are free to shout "fire" in a crowded theater. All you have to do is be prepared to accept the consequences — for example, time in jail or prison, and/or civil suits by people injured in the ensuing panic, or their survivors.

You are free to blame a madman's actions on your political adversaries. All you have to do is be prepared to accept the consequences — for example, looking like a damn fool when the madman's friends confirm he was apolitical and paid no attention to your adversaries.

Freedom comes with responsibility, accountability for your words and actions. It's not always easy to speak your mind publicly, because just as you have every right to express your views, those who hear have every right to offer their opinions in response. Sometimes other

FREEDOM AND THE BILL OF RIGHTS

people's opinions of your opinions won't be pleasant.

Never mind what Big Brother said, freedom is not slavery but rather its opposite. The solution to foolish or angry words is a reasoned response. The solution is not silencing the foolish or angry speaker by the force of new law — and the solution is certainly not violence. Not ever.

Freedom is not for the faint of heart. Freedom of speech means sometimes we will hear things we'd rather not hear. Stupid and/or evil folks will abuse freedom, and you can count on that. But the actions of a few do not justify stealing freedom from the many.

Freedom is not a gift of government. You were born with certain, inherent rights. Governments are formed to secure these rights, not create them. The most tyrannical government cannot remove these rights, although (as governments are designed to do) it may impede the exercise of freedom, and often does.

Freedom is the default mode of a human being. We relinquish our freedoms at our own peril. Think hard before you advocate for restricting any of them.

The 21st century
reaches drinking age

Here we are, past the 21st year of the 21st century. We have been in old-science-fiction-numbered years for as long as newly-minted adults have lived.

The 21st century! when all is either bright and shiny miraculous tech or long-feared dystopia and post-civilization. Can it be both? Surely. Much of what readers are reading these days is post-apocalyptic, stories of life after some manmade or natural-but-caused-by-man disaster that Earth is trying to heal from.

Of course, as all good science fiction always has been, the stories are really about who we are now, what 100-200-500 years from now will look like if we stay this course, and how humans will interact in that world.

No, not "will," rather "could." A wise editor once

taught me not to declare that something "will" happen: If you write, "The county fair will be held next month" and the county fair is canceled for whatever reason, circumstances have made you a liar or at least inaccurate. Better to write, "The county fair is scheduled to be held on these dates," and now your journalism is accurate.

So when we say the future "will" be a tech nightmare where people are oppressed and history is erased, or when we say the future "will" have books burning, or when we say the future "will" have spaceships with hundreds of people inside exploring new worlds and new civilizations — those are only things that "could" happen.

We have the ability to, well, accept the things we cannot change and change the things we can. Now we just need to muster the serenity and the courage and the wisdom to move forward. The real future will be somewhere between utopia and dystopia, as it always has been. Or should I say it "could" be?

Hold these truths:
The First Amendment

"Congress shall make no law respecting an establishment of religion, or prohibiting the free exercise thereof; or abridging the freedom of speech, or of the press, or the right of the people peaceably to assemble, and to petition the Government for a redress of grievances."

Given the impunity with which these prohibitions have been ignored in the last 20 to 100 years, I think it's safe to say most every "duly elected" official we know ought to be removed for violating the oath to defend the Constitution, but just assuming for a second this is still the supreme law of the land, let's make an observation or several.

· The author(s) of this amendment wrote, first, belief in a higher power and how you peaceably practice that belief is none of the gummint's damn business.

· The gummint can't tell anyone to shut up their mouths, no matter if anyone is talking balderdash, perceived balderdash, or even hate.

· The gummint can't regulate what anyone publishes — and ohbytheway, this applies to stuff that isn't published on paper since the definition of "press" has evolved to include publishers of stuff on radio waves, TV signals, digital means and all sorts of once-unimaginable conveyances.

· There are no "unlesses" in this amendment. It just refers to the right peaceably to assemble, for example, and doesn't limit that right by race, creed, sex, age, or say, if there's a virus afoot on the land. Anyone who said gummint has the right to shut down coffeehouses, theaters, or even stadiums just doesn't know how to read.

· I haven't seen any attempt to deny people's right to petition the gummint for a redress of grievances. I just haven't seen the gummint paying any no mind to people's rights or grievances.

· Corporations that receive special favors from the gummint are de facto extensions of said gummint. Therefore, when, for example, a social media corporation shuts down free speech, it too is violating the First Amendment. It lost its "private entity and therefore entitled to its own rules" status when it got in bed with "public entities."

· I have no illusion that the rights supposedly protected under the First Amendment are being protected at all, or that by stating this fact the gummint or its "private sector partners" will change anything they're up to. I just want to remind people — or inform them if they were unaware:

The First Amendment, like the following nine amendments, does not create these rights. It simply forbids the abridgment of these pre-existing rights.

A modest proposal

I propose that we, the people, begin to enforce these 10 steps to bring our runaway government under control.

1. Congress shall make no law respecting an establishment of religion, or prohibiting the free exercise thereof; or abridging the freedom of speech, or of the press; or the right of the people peaceably to assemble, and to petition the government for a redress of grievances.

2. A well regulated militia, being necessary to the security of a free state, the right of the people to keep and bear arms, shall not be infringed.

3. No soldier shall, in time of peace be quartered in any house, without the consent of the owner, nor in time of war, but in a manner to be prescribed by law.

4. The right of the people to be secure in their

persons, houses, papers, and effects, against unreasonable searches and seizures, shall not be violated, and no warrants shall issue, but upon probable cause, supported by oath or affirmation, and particularly describing the place to be searched, and the persons or things to be seized.

5. No person shall be held to answer for a capital, or otherwise infamous crime, unless on a presentment or indictment of a grand jury, except in cases arising in the land or naval forces, or in the militia, when in actual service in time of war or public danger; nor shall any person be subject for the same offense to be twice put in jeopardy of life or limb; nor shall be compelled in any criminal case to be a witness against himself, nor be deprived of life, liberty, or property, without due process of law; nor shall private property be taken for public use, without just compensation.

6. In all criminal prosecutions, the accused shall enjoy the right to a speedy and public trial, by an impartial jury of the state and district wherein the crime shall have been committed, which district shall have

been previously ascertained by law, and to be informed of the nature and cause of the accusation; to be confronted with the witnesses against him; to have compulsory process for obtaining witnesses in his favor, and to have the assistance of counsel for his defense.

7. In suits at common law, where the value in controversy shall exceed twenty dollars, the right of trial by jury shall be preserved, and no fact tried by a jury, shall be otherwise reexamined in any court of the United States, than according to the rules of the common law.

8. Excessive bail shall not be required, nor excessive fines imposed, nor cruel and unusual punishments inflicted.

9. The enumeration in the Constitution, of certain rights, shall not be construed to deny or disparage others retained by the people.

10. The powers not delegated to the United States by the Constitution, nor prohibited by it to the states, are reserved to the states respectively, or to the people.

Love for the Nine and Ten

A long time ago in a blogosphere far, far away, I attempted a series reviewing the Bill of Rights, one amendment at a time, to show how each had been abused over the years. I abandoned the project after six installments, in part because I began to see how much I still needed to learn about the history, and in part because the exercise was so discouraging.

None of the first 10 constitutional amendments gets anything more than lip service these days, and after years of disuse, some of them do not even have popular support.

The ninth and 10th tenets of the Bill of Rights (L. Neil Smith argued it should have been named the more accurate "Bill of Limitations") are especially swept under the carpet in any discussion of "constitutional rights," also a misnomer because the Constitution is not the source of rights; rather it is a list of some of the rights that the gummint has no fricking right to curtail. People's rights are, as eloquently stated in the country's founding document, "certain, unalienable," and "endowed by their Creator."

To drive home that point, Amendments Nine and Ten declare, "The enumeration in the Constitution of certain rights shall not be construed to deny or disparage others retained by the people," and "The powers not delegated to the United States by the Constitution, nor prohibited by it to the States, are reserved to the States respectively, or to the people."

In other words, this list of people's rights is just a bunch of things the federal government can't infringe, and oh by the way, if we didn't mention any particular certain unalienable right here, then that authority may (or may not) be assumed by the separate states, and if the state doesn't want to curtail that right, then the people are free to have at it.

You say something "is not in the Constitution"? Oh yes, it is, right here in Amendments Nine and Ten.

That's where it says specifically, "Hands off, feds, that ain't none of your business, either."

Now, of course, a lot of this was changed between 1861 and 1865, when a war was waged in part over whether states have a right to go their separate ways, and the central government declared it had the power to overrule any such notion. But the discussion continues to this day.

Once upon a time, the words "state" and "country" were somewhat interchangeable. The original idea, I believe you'll find, as that the 13 former colonies formed a federation of independent nations; you might have called it the United Nations. That's why you'll find references to some of the Founders being "Virginians," for example, rather than "Americans."

Only after a very long time did the notion emerge that these united countries were actually one big hairy country. Breaking away would be like if one of the nations in the European Union decided it didn't want to participate anymore and the EU moved heaven and earth to try to prevent such a secession. At least they didn't go to war over it in these more civilized times.

It behooves those of us who still read the Bill of Limitations to be more active in pointing out, "You can't do that" or, at least, "You're not supposed to be able to do that," whenever Congress or some more petty dictator makes a move that violates the principles. The exhausting part of that endeavor, of course, is that both the individual states and the Federation have gone so far beyond the limits that a day doesn't pass without violations galore.

Still, it couldn't hurt to start asking, for example, "What part of 'shall not' do you folks not understand?" or even examine those words "delegated" and "prohibited" in the Tenth Amendment. Because as I have always understood those words, the higher power is not vested in Washington but in 50 other cities scattered here and there with names like Trenton and Pierre and Cheyenne and (God help us) Sacramento. And from the very first words — "We the People" — we get our best sense of who exactly is supposed to be doing the delegating and prohibiting.

ECHOES OF FREEDOM PAST

Maybe the horse has been out of the barn for so long that it's had time to procreate many generations of horses, but maybe it wouldn't do much harm (and maybe could help a little) to start chasing down that horse and see what can be done about reining it back in.

It's all on us

I got up on the wrong side of the bed this morning. Everything irritated me. Except I got up on the same side of the bed I always do. What was the real difference? Why was it that little things I usually overlook were now annoying? What was the — to use a silly overused psycho word — trigger?

It had been a night of interesting, even entertaining dreams. I have no actual recollection of the content, just that I was engaged in the stories and a willing participant. There may even have been a happy ending, and maybe therein is a clue. I didn't want to leave that world and wake up to this complicated world with its foolish idiots trying to run our lives and its words my failing ears can't hear and its dogs that demand attention and the new crossword puzzle in the local paper that I can't solve without over-reliance on my cheat website.

It's all in the attitude, they say. We can't help that politicians are almost uniformly sociopaths who commit evil because they can't help themselves. We can't help that wars are started to change the subject from their incompetence, and people die to cover up their mistakes. We can't help that the sun isn't shining or we're out of breakfast cereal or the film we watched last night had a stupid ending.

The only thing we can help is our reaction and how we process what happened.

I have to say, that realization does make it easier to let go of the irritable feelings. I remember I love our home and all its denizens and that life is pretty good here. I remember that as much as they want to be the center of our lives and bombard us with reasons "why they need us," they really don't affect our everyday lives substantially and we're free to live more or less as we wish.

Why are petty thieves and villains in charge of the world? They're not. Petty thieves and villains are in charge of the world's governments, but the governments are not the world and the governments are not "us." When governors and their governments act, we didn't do that; the alleged bosses of our lives did. Oh yes, when we blindly obey or do what they say, we did do that, but they don't represent us when they go about their everyday madness.

I have no quarrel with you; I just want to live my life my way and let you live your life your way and beg pardon when we go different ways, as long as we don't infringe on each other. I saw a quote from John Wayne's last movie, *The Shootist*, the other day, in which his character said, "I won't be wronged, I won't be insulted, I won't be laid a hand on. I don't do these things to other people, and I require the same of them." I must say that's a lovely way to live, if stated a mite harshly. Essentially it's "Be kind and expect kindness, and you'll get up on the right side of the bed more often."

ZAPping our way to freedom

I believe I became a kinder, gentler man when I stumbled across the Zero Aggression Principle, or ZAP, best articulated by the recently deceased L. Neil Smith: "No one has the right, under any circumstances, to initiate force against another human being for any reason whatever; nor should anyone advocate the initiation of force, or delegate it to anyone else."

That principle says what I have always believed and how I think most people live their lives. At a young age I admired the U.S. government's rebranding of its War Department as the Department of Defense and its declaration that it would never initiate a first strike in an armed conflict. I liked the concept that violence would only be used defensively. (Part of my later disillusionment with government was when I realized both the rebranding and the declaration were dishonest, but that's for another day.)

I always admired Smith's writing. He was forceful, clear and effective in stating his views, which were passionately held and had the Zero Aggression Principle at their core. But I had never read any of his books, and so on hearing of his death I sought to rectify that oversight and am now in possession of and thirstily reading *The Probability Broach*, his first and most well-known novel, and *Lever Action*, a 2000 collection of his articles, speeches and letters to the editor that another person I respect recently cited as life-changing.

The latter collection was delivered a perfect day because I had time to read for a while and the puppy fell asleep on my foot, forcing me to do nothing but page through the first 60 or so pages.

And I realized something I always knew instinctively but never quite verbalized: The linchpin word in ZAP is "initiate." The principle does not eschew force or violence; it eschews the *initiation* of force or violence. As I said, I always knew that, I just downplayed it because I so much admire those who seek and choose nonviolent solutions.

Smith was an ardent proponent of the Second Amendment — all 10 amendments that comprise the Bill of Rights, in fact. The book begins with a 1994 speech he gave advocating a society where those 10 limitations on government were sacred and enforced. The Second Amendment is about the individual's right to use violence in self-defense, nothing more, nothing less.

Such a society — with the Bill of Rights summarized in the Zero Aggression Principle — would necessarily be kinder and gentler, Smith argued, and I agree. If we all agreed never to initiate violence on one another — and tacitly agreed that violence initiated would be met in kind — then the impulse to turn to violence would be under control most of the time.

Over and over in his 1994 speech Smith repeated a pledge he said should be required of all public servants, who would be subject to arrest if they ever violated it — and of course the administration running the country at that time would be rounded up first thing: "I swear by my life, my fortune, and my sacred honor to uphold the first 10 Amendments to the Constitution of the United States, popularly known as the 'Bill of Rights.'"

What a different world we would live in, if we made our rulers adhere to that pledge. We owe it to ourselves, and to the memory of L. Neil Smith, to get started.

ECHOES OF FREEDOM PAST

Our present crisis

ECHOES OF FREEDOM PAST

A flock of squirrels

Our attention has been redirected so many times in the last few years that a pandemic of whiplash may be the next national panic.

As soon as we start sniffing the ground for a whiff of what really ails us, the Powers That Be shout "Squirrel!" and send us scampering in another direction — until we hold up and start to think there were no rodents there, after all. And then they shout "Squirrel!" again and point thataway.

We are herded this way and that and kept off-balance so much that we miss the overarching themes.

These people hate our freedom. These people don't trust individual men and women. These people have a psychological need to keep us in line.

Who are these people? What are there motivations? It can't be simply that they are megalomaniacal tyrants,

although they act that way. They must have a reason —
and of course they will say they have our best interests
at heart, and they may actually believe that.

"Nobody puts Baby in a corner," but they sure keep
trying. If Baby squirms out of one corner, they push her
toward another. The world is full of corners until you
break out of the box.

Here, out in the sun where light outshines all
darkness, Big Brother and Big Sister are revealed as
little people the same as you and me — except you and
I don't need to force each other to act a certain way, to
hand over half our earnings, and turn over private
information, or otherwise stick our noses where they
don't belong.

There are regular folks who want to live and let live,
and there are agents of the state, a faceless quasi-
organism that purports to know best how we are to live,
and your own choices be damned. This is the real
divide, not political parties, genders, races, creeds or
however else they try to split us: The divide between
those who believe the individual should have the power

and those who believe in the state.

Some of us see a better way. Some of us stirred when we heard the words, "All are created equal, endowed with certain unalienable rights, and among these are the right to life, liberty, and the pursuit of happiness." Like the folks who signed that document, we declare independence from tyranny. We declare freedom.

The idea was revolutionary in 1776, and it remains revolutionary today. The Powers That Be responded to that declaration with a violence that continues to this day. To a certain extent the struggle feels eternal — just when you think we've made our point, The Powers That Be launch another assault on the simple desire to live and let live. It's in their nature, of course — they can't control the urge to Be That Power. The movement that generated that venerable document hoped to wrangle The Powers That Be into leaving us alone, but they just keep trying.

If we are born free, then we only become not-free when we surrender the freedom and responsibility for our own lives. And when we do, eventually we realize that no one cares about our selves, our freedoms and our well-being as much as we do, so we may as well take back our freedom and live the life we desire — as long, of course, as we respect our neighbors' right to do the same, and there, for many of us especially The Powers That Be, is the rub.

It's all about boundaries, it seems.

But they don't want us thinking in terms of freedom and individuals, so — as H.L. Mencken so aptly put it — they assail us with an endless barrage of alarming crises — hobgoblins — squirrels, if you will — to keep us running in circles while they loot.

About saying certain things

Ladies and gentlemen, honored dignitaries, and especially you graduates, I come to you as an emissary from another time, when men and women were free to come and go as they pleased.

"You're free to go" — I remember those halcyon days when this was so. If someone were to say, "How can you let someone say such things?" the most likely response would be a shrug and "It's a free country."

Voltaire was once quoted as saying — although the evidence is scant that he said this exactly — "I disapprove of what you say, but I will defend to the death your right to say it."

I remember when people said such things. How long ago was that? It seems a very long time. When did speaking your mind become so dangerous? Or was it always dangerous to say certain things, and it's only the certain things that have evolved?

We need them. Just ask them.

They want you afraid. They want you feeling hopeless. They want you to turn to them for help.

Who are "they"?

Well, who scares you? Government bosses? Drug commercials? Political commercials? Some sales guy who says his product will solve your fear?

Could be it's all of the above. It's a common tactic, and it's a common tactic because it works.

The whole idea is to alarm you and get you to search for a safe solution, which they just happen to have here for you — just $19.99 plus shipping — just tax the rich and you can have it for free —oh, and we'll need to trim just this tiny bit of your freedom to go about your business and make your own decisions.

Sometimes you just have to acknowledge that you're scared and plow ahead anyway. Everything carries a risk. When you leave the house, you might get hit by a falling meteor or held up at gunpoint. When you drive your car, some idiot might T-bone you at an intersection. When you apply for a job, you might not get it, or when you quit your job to pursue what you really want to do, you may not succeed right away. When you question government rules, regulations, guidelines or other edicts, or heaven forbid you decide not to follow them, something might happen.

With every step you take in life, you risk something going wrong.

The only safe place is in a cage. Nobody can hurt you if you're behind four sturdy walls. Ask a prison inmate alone in his cell — it's very safe in there.

They want you afraid: It makes it easier to back you into your cell. They promise this will make you safer. They never promise this will make you freer.

"Freedom is slavery anyway," they scoff. "Don't question why; ignorance is strength." And then they send us off to war in the name of peace.

Our scary science fiction present-day

Do androids dream of electric sheep, as Philip K. Dick asked?

Do smartphones dream at all? How do they know what we've been talking about so they can show us relevant ads? Oh, we know the answer to that, but we don't face the implications.

We're entertained by the pretty FBI agents on TV stalking criminals with their cellphone data and the GPS devices in their cars, and we don't tremble at the idea of constant surveillance.

Scary science fiction was written years ago about authorities watching the innocent 24 hours a day, and it was brushed off as fantasy or a future to be avoided. Now that it's a reality, we brush it off as no big deal, or even a blessing — we can be found if we get lost. And maybe if the cameras catch us doing something really embarrassing, We'll win $100,000 from *America's Funniest Home Videos.*

The ghosts of Winston Smith and Julia aren't laughing, though.

The Big Reveal
at the end of the movie

Layne splintered the door open and strode to the center of the lush office. Fitzsimmons, leaning back in his chair, raised his eyebrows slightly at the intrusion.

"I'm taking you in," the gumshoe snarled. "Can't believe it took me this long to figure it out."

"I am innocent of any foolishness you believe," the CEO said smoothly, leaning forward. "What is it you think you've figured out, old man?"

"I followed the money. I found out how you work the bribes."

"Bribes?"

"All the dirty money the politicians have been taking all these years, it got pumped into media ads."

"That has absolutely nothing to do with —"

"Just listen. So when people call for taking the dirty

money out of politics, the media ignore it. They can't lose all that revenue, they'd be cutting their own throats. You started to notice how many politicians who never worked an honest job were buying second and third homes."

"You're still not connecting any dots to me or my company."

"OK, dot this. You used to have an army of sales reps going from doctor to doctor peddling your newest drugs, but it was taking too long to get rich and you had to pay all those reps, so you greased some politicians to make selling medicine on TV legal again. You fired the reps and turned the patients into your sales force. 'Ask your doctor if this pill is right for you. Oh, it could kill you, but you'll feel better and your skin will clear up.'"

"Oh, puh-leeze —"

"But that wasn't enough. You wanted it all. So you and the state got married — you sell them the drugs, they give them out 'free,' and they make it a law to take them. Why not, it's free, and you and your family could die if you don't."

"Are you serious? We're saving lives here."

"You're getting filthy rich, filthier and richer than you ever imagined, and the media watchdogs — what a laugh — they're laying down and shutting up anyone who's onto you because politicians and drug companies are their two biggest sources of income."

"This — conspiracy theory — is what you 'figured out after all this time'? These absurd lies and misinformation? You foolish man."

"I'm bringing you in, Fitzsimmons. The game's over."

The man at the desk began to chuckle.

"Oh, I don't think so." He pressed a button.

Three burly men entered the room.

+ + + + +

"...And that's the real story," the homeless man told the reporter. "Next thing I knew, I was out of a job and on the street. No one would believe me, or if they did, they didn't have the guts to buck Big Pharma and the state."

"That's a lot of — I don't know what it is, but it's a

lot of something," said the reporter. "You got any proof, any documents, any shred of evidence?"

"It was all in my computer and my files," the raggedy man said. "Erased and burned long ago, I suppose."

"Right. Well, I can't take this to my editors like this. It would make sense to the conspiracy nuts, but you have one thing right — all those drug and political ads pay my salary."

"And to hell with the truth, right?"

"That IS the truth," the reporter said. "People gotta eat. Gotta feed the family."

"Yeah, tell me about it," the disgraced cop said. "Maybe I just thought I'd let you know what kind of people are paying your salary."

"I guess I've always known," the reporter said. "But it's bigger than us. And I do like knowing where my next meal is coming from."

"I hear you," said the homeless man, turning to the door. "Have a nice life, and remember to take your pills."

Thoreau was onto something

"I saw that the state was half-witted ..."

Resistance to Civil Government: On the Duty of Civil Disobedience has proven over the years to be the most consistent seller among the books in my little stable of tomes. Perhaps because its message is a timeless one that resonates through the centuries.

"I heartily accept the motto, 'that government is best which governs least,' and I should like to see it acted up to more rapidly and systematically. Carried out, it finally amounts to this, which also I believe: 'That government is best which governs not at all.'"

Boom. There it is.

A dystopia, if they can keep it

Benjamin Franklin, who famously said that the Founders had crafted "a republic, if you can keep it," is also often quoted (apparently incorrectly) as saying those who would trade their freedom for a small measure of security will have neither.

H.L. Mencken did write, and I often quote, "The whole aim of practical politics is to keep the populace alarmed (and hence clamorous to be led to safety) by an endless series of hobgoblins, most of them imaginary."

I picked up my 50th anniversary edition of *Animal Farm* the other day, and found in the 1996 preface — and to a certain extent, even the reprinted 1954 introduction — a sense of relief that the world had escaped the dystopian Soviet model that so concerned George Orwell when he wrote his brilliant fairy story in the 1940s. I'm not so sure that their relief was justified.

ECHOES OF FREEDOM PAST

The events of Sept. 11, 2001, and the COVID-19 virus in 2020 have given the hobgoblin manipulators unprecedented opportunities to push individual rights under their thumbs.

And now we wait for Big Brother to give us permission to walk outside, to exchange goods, to embrace a dying loved one. It's the virus, they would like us to believe, that suddenly crashed the economy, not the politicians with their political motives and machinations. Before this, it was the terrorists who forced authorities to search innocents' personal belongings, put cameras in every nook and cranny, and monitor our communications and bank accounts.

Fear has always been the politicians' greatest tool. Advertisers will try to create a nagging itch to convince you to buy their products. But the politician takes that to the next level, tapping into our ever-present fear of death and making us "clamorous to be led to safety."

In Orwell's cautionary tales, all animals are created equal, but some animals are more equal than others. In his master work, *Nineteen Eighty-Four,* the author created a world of newspeak and thought crimes, where people sincerely believe that suppression of certain opinions and ideologies is necessary to protect and preserve. In our new real world, the rulers have no need for a Ministry of Propaganda when they have social media and alleged journalists willing to carry out the suppression of dissent.

Ray Bradbury in *Fahrenheit 451* wrote that it wasn't necessary for the government to ban books when people in general clamored to burn them. Aldous Huxley in *Brave New World* wrote of an entire society so sedated on pills, bread and circuses that they didn't notice how thoroughly they were being manipulated.

The literature of Dystopia will be harder to write now that we live there.

All is not lost. I write these words for you fairly confident that I won't be arrested by the end of the day. I don't expect to be "disappeared" after posting this, never to be heard from again.

These are scary times, but as one of the cleverest of those practical politicians once said, fear itself is the biggest problem. Fear makes people do such foolish things. We will survive and even conquer the forces of dystopia if we are willing to overcome our legitimate fears and live as free men and women, taking such precautions as necessary to avoid the occasional hobgoblin that is not imaginary. (And yes, COVID-19 is real enough.)

My goal here is to persuade you to control your fears, get out there and live your life.

Reclaiming and restoring liberty

ECHOES OF FREEDOM PAST

An election party
where nobody came

(Written in the fall of 2008, and still valid every four years.)

Well, it's been a quiet week in Freedomville, my hometown ... I sense a disturbance in the Force, or something. It's an uneasiness in a soul that has chosen not to participate in the charade we call a "presidential election." Or the anxiety, if that's the right word, is something other than that.

The discomfort must be something more than resigning myself to the fact that the two branches of the Party have presented the US of A with finalists in the presidential reality show who each proposes to be the dictator of our lives, improving only the efficiency of a safety net woven from chains that purports to protect us from cradle to grave while regulating, licensing or prohibiting nearly every known individual choice or course of action. Maybe it's something as easy as realizing that everyone who was voted off the island was also anxious to be our dictator.

But this is nothing new. Perhaps it's that this is my first "presidential election" since my disillusionment in this process became complete. I have reported to a polling place and voted for the Libertarian Party candidate for four of the last five of these exercises, which gave me some sense of empowerment. I never bought into the "if you vote for a third party, you've wasted your vote" nonsense. I have always said that if you vote for someone who doesn't share your values or views in any meaningful sense of the words, THEN you've wasted your vote. It's not about winning, it's about representation, and if the numbers show your viewpoints aren't representative, your views will be ignored. Or so I believed.

Now it seems clear that my views will be ignored anyway. And so I will join the majority that votes

"None of the Above," who is not on the ballot. I have seen unopposed candidates fret because they received only 94 percent of the vote, wondering how they could have disillusioned as many as 6 percent. So I know the fewer people vote, the more it will get the attention of our rulers. The fewer people vote, the more it will trouble good men and women.

The dilemma is it's also true that the fewer people vote, the easier it is for a devious minority to maintain control, because all you need is 50.1 percent of a small minority to win the election. That's a motivation for voting for the "lesser of two evils." But the better choice between two evils is still evil. The only sane choice is neither, not one or the other.

I know and understand all of this, so why do I sense a disturbance in my heart? I wonder if it's something as basic as finally understanding to the core that the extent to which I am free has nothing to do with politics, nothing to do with the chains so many freely choose. The extent to which I am free is up to me. The extent to which I have not been free was my responsibility.

ECHOES OF FREEDOM PAST

Freedom is not something granted by rulers; it's an "unalienable right" that I have given away.

How do I get back my freedom? First I understand that I never lost it, I merely chose not to be free. How do I get back my freedom? I take it back, gently but firmly. One small step is to note that neither Barack Obama nor John McCain represents me in any way, shape or form. Freedom is not about having the right ruler. Oh, wait, yes it is. Freedom is understanding that I am the boss of me.

Take back your life

(With hat tips to The Outer Limits *and Freddie Mercury.)*

We live in a time of seemingly unprecedented privacy invasion, government overreach, and Orwellian illogic.

These wannabe overlords are far less relevant than they imagine.

You control the reception of their messages. If you wish to make it louder, you can bring up the volume. If you wish to make it softer, you can tune it to a whisper. You control the horizontal. You control the vertical. You can roll the image, make it flutter. You can change the focus to a soft blur or sharpen it to crystal clarity.

In the big picture, on the bottom line, at the end of the day, you control all that you see and hear. You are participating in a great adventure, experiencing the awe and mystery that reaches from the inner mind to the outer limits.

ECHOES OF FREEDOM PAST

It's not theirs to control, no matter what the voice in the little box is telling you. Open your eyes, look up to the skies, and see.

The only free dog on this train

When Summer the 9-month-old puppy goes outside, either she is tethered to a leash or the area where she roams is surrounded by fencing, for her protection.

She loves foraging for sticks and leaves. We are still fearful because eight years ago her older sister, Dejah, needed emergency surgery at age 2 months because she ate so many sticks and twigs and pebbles and mulch that it threatened to damage her system.

So when Summer picks up a stick in her mouth, we chastise her. "Leave it!" We say sternly.

Usually, she lies down and starts chewing on the stick, a defiant look in her eye.

"Leave it!" we cry again. She drops one stick and picks up another.

"OK, back in the house!" we might insist.

She will skulk toward the house and, just before

reaching the porch, she snatches a leaf from the ground and carries it into the house.

Summer is the only free dog on this train.

What darkness?

It's all in our minds, you know.

This world, this existence, this life, is all so breathtakingly beautiful that we are overcome.

And so, we find ways to reduce the enormity.

We glaze our eyes over.

We divert our attention.

We fuss among ourselves.

We deliberately seek ugliness, and darkness, and what hurts.

And so, we miss the obvious.

This is obviously a huge, beautiful world in a universe of infinite and unspeakable grandeur.

Our minds can scarcely drink it all in, so we try to make the universe smaller.

We try to make it less grand.

We focus on the imperfections.

ECHOES OF FREEDOM PAST

We focus on the petty differences.

When we lift our eyes, however, we know the meaning of awe.

It is too much, until it is just enough.

Then, and only then, do we see.

Life is not a small, churlish thing.

Life is a big, wide adventure full of wonder, that is to say, wonderful.

The more we wonder, the more we live.

The more we live, the more we chase the dark away.

Light bright lights along the path, the better to heal the darkness.

Anthem

There is such beauty in the world, such innocence, so much that is miraculous.

It's almost criminal that we focus on anything but.

We log onto social media spoiling for a fight, daring the rest of the world to offend us.

We fill the airwaves with the latest reports of humanity's inhumanity.

"Be afraid. Be very afraid. The sky is not falling today, but the forecast is grim for the weekend."

Why not seek out peace? Why not see the yearning for comfort in the eyes of the people who disagree with us but, in the end, are just as human as our own families?

I can be as outraged as the next person. After all, we're being ruled by people who think *Nineteen Eighty-Four* has a happy ending. "He loved Big Brother," after all. Isn't that the goal?

ECHOES OF FREEDOM PAST

I would rather learn from one puppy how to love chasing leaves in the wind, than teach a thousand sheep how to toe the line.

Go follow the puppy.

The times they are ridiculous

It's been eight years since I posted this on Facebook in April 2014:

"There's an old Chinese curse, 'May you live in interesting times.' I'm not sure about interesting, but I'm beginning to think we live in ridiculous times."

I watch the social media go by, and I watch the politicians do their dance, and I watch and I watch and I watch.

And the more I watch, the more I think I nailed it eight years ago.

There's nothing wrong with the world that couldn't be helped by a good belly laugh.

Wouldn't it be great if someone, in the middle of a huge argument or a heated battle or a self-righteous declaration, just waved their arms and said, "Wait, wait, wait. You know what? This is ridiculous!"

Emerging From Dystopia

An article making the rounds the other day noted that Ray Bradbury predicted all this, writing in his dystopian classic *Fahrenheit 451*, that people would demand tyranny and censorship, that it would not be forced upon us but enforced by popular demand. Yes, Bradbury's book does contain that bleakness.

But —

But *Fahrenheit 451* ends with hope, with Granger talking about a silly damn bird called a Phoenix that burned itself up every few hundred years and then got himself born all over again, adding that we're the same but we've got one thing the Phoenix didn't have: the ability to remember all the silly damn things we've done, and as long as we know that and remember, some day we'll stop making the goddam funeral pyres and jumping in the middle of them.

"And some day we'll remember so much that we'll build the biggest goddam steamshovel in history and dig the biggest grave of all time and shove war in and cover it up. Come on now, we're going to go build a mirror-factory first and put out nothing but mirrors for the next year and take a long look in them."

Every generation has people who remember and preserve the lessons and whisper encouragement to the peacemakers. Every generation we gain a few more who remember, and oh so quietly the biggest goddam steamshovel in history is being assembled, and someday someone is going to stop before he throws a punch or a Molotov cocktail or burns a book, and he'll say to himself, "How stupid is this?"

Sometime after the end of *Fahrenheit 451*, someone found an old printing press and dusted it off and oiled it up and started making books, a little at a time, and people taught each other how to read them and write them and start to understand each other again.

That's the difference between this novel and the other great dystopian works — *Nineteen Eighty-four* and

ECHOES OF FREEDOM PAST

Brave New World have bleak endings, the individual crushed by Big Brother and the gaping foolishness of society, but Fahrenheit 451 ends with hope, because Bradbury saw the potential in the heart of humanity. He looked up and saw the stars.

o o o o o

And what else will people remember?

That all are created equal, endowed by their Creator with certain, unalienable rights, including the right to life, the right to liberty, and the right to pursue happiness. "Endowed by their Creator," not by the bosses, rights that were ours from the moment of creation, rights we have held since birth, and let no tyrant try to take them away. He or she may send armies to lock you down, but they cannot crush your rights without your permission.

In dystopia, no one talks about freedom. But some remember. They hold the memory delicately like a flower that might be crushed, but freedom is not so fragile. Freedom is baked into our DNA and forged into our souls. Our instinct to be free is slapped and shoved and slashed and burned, but it is impervious to all.

"They may take our lives, but they will never take our freedom." It's a line in a movie, spoken by a character who lived and died 700 years ago. In another film a man is chained for calling out liars among their wannabe rulers, and he rattles the handcuff and declares, "I am the only free man on this train."

In the stories, those men died, but we remember them, and we remember what they said.

o o o o o

There was an empire and an emperor, and neither could see faces; they only saw the people, and they treated the people as if they were their children, and they taught the people to serve the emperor and the empire, but they never saw the faces, they only saw the mass, and they didn't see that inside that mass were infinite numbers of faces, and many were hurting, and many suffered.

But one day, a person stood up and said, "I have an idea." And another called back, "I've had that idea, too." And others said, "Yes, and here's another idea." And all of them had faces. That was how it began, you see: That was how people began to stop thinking of themselves as "the masses" and began to see each other.

They realized that there was no single, amorphous mass, only a great number of individuals with the ability to work together in harmony, each of them so powerful that a proverb said, "When an old person dies, a library burns to the ground." When they understood that the true power resides inside each individual, the false and manufactured power of the empire began to fade, until it came to pass that everyone understood the emperor was simply another individual, no greater or lesser than any other of us.

Darkness descends, and night may last a very long time, but some of us remember and whisper about the light and the promise and the face of hope. That may not be much, but some day it will be enough.

RECLAIMING AND RESTORING LIBERTY

o o o o o

Post-apocalyptic literature assumes that a cataclysm of some kind is the inevitable climax to dystopia — but catastrophe is always avoidable, until it isn't. A series of choices makes the situation worse and worse until Big Brother micromanages lives (*Nineteen Eighty-Four*) or the populace lives in a drugged stupor (*Brave New World*) or people demand books be banned or even burned (*Fahrenheit 451*), or all of the above (2020).

But it doesn't have to end with scorched earth, until, of course, the landscape is scorched. At any time before that, the disaster can be avoided.

In *Fahrenheit 451*, the earth is scorched, but there's a sense that we will rebuild. This is scant consolation to those who must do the work of rebuilding, of moving from scorched earth to Eden, but it is better than inconsolable.

The challenge is finding a way to avoid the cataclysm, to stop short of Ragnarok and move straight to Eden, ending the dystopia without the devastation.

In the context of the upcoming election, there is little hope of emerging from dystopia anytime in the short term. Both major parties intend to maintain the surveillance culture, continue the restrictions on freedom that have been building for more than a generation, and wield the power of Leviathan against individuals who don't toe the line.

But those who remember freedom need not abandon hope. Support exists for a culture where alternative views may be voiced and heard openly and in peace. Many are weary of the military industrial complex's grip on the tiller. Many more, who want nothing more than to live at peace with their neighbors, are weary of being micromanaged by so-called leaders who think they know better. As The Powers That Be attempt to tighten the stranglehold, people still wish to come and go and they please, and to live their own lives.

We may or may not avoid the apocalypse, but many people yearn for something other than dystopia. Big Brother is an unsustainable concept. At some point totalitarianism must crumble, because its grip can never be total. The State cannot control millions and billions of individual lives against their free will. The Soviet Union collapsed. The Third Reich was a blip on history, a horrid abominable blip but gone in hardly a decade.

People get tired of living in fear. At some point they look the fear in the eye and say, "Shut up. Enough. We're going to live our lives. Try and stop us if you want, but you'll fail. Fear is not the boss of me."

I've got a bell and a song to sing

"In the folk classic 'If I Had A Hammer,' the hammer represents justice, one of these freedom."

The answer to the Jeopardy! question was a no-brainer. "Bell," I said to the air. "The bell of freedom." Next question.

But wait, the three contestants — none of whom looked old enough to have been alive in 1962 or 1963, to be fair — stared into space with confused looks on their faces.

As happens at times like these, I said to the air, a little louder, "Bell! The bell of freedom! Really?!?!?" And the time buzzer went off.

"Bell," said Ken Jennings, hosting, "the bell of freedom."

I guess they don't sing about freedom these days. Why would we want young people to sing about freedom?

Do they even know what freedom is or what freedom feels like?

A generation doesn't know what it's like not to be surveilled and monitored at every turn. They don't worry if someone's listening because someone is always listening, even if it's just the AI on the nearest electronic device.

They don't know what it's like to get on a plane without being treated like a criminal suspect. If someone in authority tells them to lock themselves in their homes, they stay home.

Come to think of it, there's one more item in the song that the kids ought to be taught to sing about.

"I've got a hammer, and I've got a bell, and I've got a song to sing all over this land," the last verse of the song goes. "It's the hammer of justice, it's the bell of freedom, *it's a song about love between my brothers and my sisters all over this land.*"

There's still talk about justice these days, but freedom? and wait a minute, love?! When there are people in that other party to shut up and people in those other countries to kill? What the heck kind of a song is that, anyway?

I think maybe it's a song that needs to be sung and taught to our kids, so that when that episode of Jeopardy! is rerun, everyone watching will yell at the screen, "Bell! It's the bell of freedom!!"

A few words about gratitude
Thanksgiving Day 2021

This is the day, here in the U.S. of A., where people spend some time talking and writing about how thankful they are, and a few million turkeys are consumed in a grand spirit of gratitude.

I've seen several social media friends get caught up in a challenge to write something they're grateful for for 10 consecutive days or more, notwithstanding that it's not the fourth Thursday in November.

It's a healthy thing to be thankful. It's a healthy thing to express gratitude. Scientific studies show that thankful people live longer and have cuter puppies. Or something like that.

I don't know whether the scientific thing is real, but I do know I feel much better when I turn my thoughts toward reasons to be thankful, as opposed to thinking about reasons to be resentful or angry or sad or discouraged.

In a world where The Powers That Be seem hellbent on making people scared and unhappy and resentful, I am thankful that growing numbers of people see through the silliness and decide they're going to be thankful and love their neighbors anyway.

I am grateful to be alive in this amazing era where I can make a few clicks with a keyboard and reach people thousands of miles away. I am thankful that there is a person and non-human family members within reach as I type this. I am grateful to be on this amazing world full of life. I am thankful to be able to look up in the sky at night and see a universe.

Life is too precious, and life is too short, to spend so much time being anything but awestruck.

Beyond 'Refuse to be Afraid'

"They" have always wanted "us" to be afraid, and they've stepped up their game the past two years. It's harder than ever to refuse to be afraid: "They" have "us" questioning every sniffle and worrying about every cough.

The intensity of it all is enough to make a person angry. Some of the fear mongering is downright infuriating. And so many silly people are taking up the call on antisocial media, a person could stay angry all the time.

And that brings up a question: What if "they" WANT "us" to stay angry? Why would "they" want "us" angry all the time? Well, people act stupid when they're afraid, but they act even stupider when they're afraid and angry.

It's been obvious for years that "they" prefer "us" to

be fearful; it's much easier to manipulate scared people. But if they can also scare us into anger, maybe we will do some of their dirty work for them, like shun or censor or even injure or kill people who refuse to be fearful or kowtowed.

What if people refused to be afraid AND refused to get angry? It would be a lot harder to manipulate "us."

Unafraid and calm people can see through clouds of bullshit, and Powers That Be who can't fool or manipulate people are, well, powerless.

I begin to believe the key to getting through the BS barrage is to keep your fear in check and don't get angry. A good laugh at their expense is also helpful.

For years I've preached "Refuse to be Afraid." I even wrote a book about it: *Refuse to be Afraid. Free yourself. Dream.* In these "challenging" times, the exhortation has an important corollary:

Refuse to be Angry.

Recall the old expression, "Don't get mad, get even." It's an ominous expression, because it seems to advocate cold, calculated revenge — but cold calculation is better than rage. When you're not blinded by anger, you can think things through.

How do you check anger at the door? "Count to 10." Do something, anything, that focuses your mind on not lashing back in a rage.

Stop long enough to consider: Why does this person want you angry? Again, angry people do stupid things without thinking — seeking an eye for an eye, for example — and they do stuff that could provide a handy excuse to, say, arrest the angry person, perhaps lock him away for a long, long time.

Just as wondering why "they" want "us" to be afraid leads to insights about the nature of government and politics and advertising and such, it can be educational to wonder why "they" want "us" to be angry. Like the fear monger, the rabble rouser seeks to control and/or to manipulate. The fearful will often shut down in paralysis; the rager needs an outlet, and with a little finesse the anger can be directed and more or less controlled.

When on the verge of being paralyzed by fear or

blinded by rage, the best course is often to step back and ask those questions.

Ask: Why are you doing this? Why are you trying to scare me? Why are you trying to get me angry? What is your agenda? What do you want?

What DO "they" want? What good is a scared and raging mob?

I feel like I sound paranoid, but I sincerely wonder who benefits when fear and anger washes over antisocial media and newscasts day after day. Surely, rulers and pretenders to the throne benefit when we are afraid of each other and when we are angry at our neighbors. The more we shun and/or fight among ourselves, the less attention we pay to who is pulling the strings.

I have a new theme, piled on top of the old theme.

Refuse to be Angry.

Quit your raging

The extent to which rage has become a common ingredient in politics (and spilling over into everyday life) is uncanny. It's well documented how anger eats at your mind, your body, your very soul, and yet so much rhetoric is expended building rage.

Spend a few minutes reviewing the words of the average practicing politician of any stripe, and you will either find an angry man or woman, or you will hear words intended to make you angry.

Imagine if our chief export was peace.

Imagine if all the energy people channel into their rage was instead applied to love and mercy and trying to understand.

Imagine if, instead of expending fury, we fought just as hard to love our neighbors and smile on a brother.

ECHOES OF FREEDOM PAST

In the end, the battle belongs to love. The ultimate triumph goes not to the one who shouted the loudest, whose hate was fiercest, whose arms were most powerful. No, victory belongs to the one who spoke most gently, whose love was most unshakable, and whose arms reached out in support.

Rage, a cousin of fear, is a disease that seeks to burn all in its path. Love will hold up the universe if need be.

At Christmas: Study war no more

It's ironic, in a world of constant war and gleeful hatred wherever we turn, that our most sacred holidays celebrate the birth, death and resurrection of a man whose coming was heralded with angels singing, "Peace on Earth, good will toward men."

Every so often, and especially around Christmas, we pause and consider the new testament Jesus brought, with God's law condensed to two commandments: Love the Lord your God, and Love One Another. How's that working out for us?

One of these days we really are going to lay our burdens down and study war no more.

I see members of the ruling class badmouthing each other and rattling sabers, safe in the knowledge that they're not the ones who will have to wield the sabers if push comes to shove, and I despair that a day of peace on Earth will ever come.

But then I see strangers smile at each other, I hear children laughing together, and I feel the emotion in a song everyone loves, I see all kinds of people working and playing together, and I remember that we have more in common than we have differences. The political class have to work hard to keep us driven apart.

If we could keep the spirit that pervades this season and make it 24/7/365 ... what a world that could be.

A vision of smoke and mirrors

I opened my eyes and saw a vast plain of people climbing over each other, scratching and clawing and seeking approval and validation, looking for love in all the wrong places, people talking without speaking and hearing without listening, a crowd lost in their loneliness, and a monolith in the middle that they struggled to touch, to worship, to — what's that word where you follow blindly without realizing you're following anything? They made a great din of absolute quiet, and I choked back my fear and turned away.

A little while later I could still hear the shouting and braying of donkeys and elephants, nary an eagle nor a lion among them, and the farm animals fattening themselves up to be eaten, but I was walking across a barren field searching for green against the beige. Not the beige of a desert or late autumn, just a plain of dried mud, no moisture, no nourishment to be found — arid and empty and what has become of the land that was made for you and me?

This cacophony of silence, this celebration of despair, and where is this coming from? I know gladness is infectious, I seek hope in all things, I see the light in the darkness, and yet the mob screams nothing and their contagion creeps into the corners of my mind.

Am I some naive gump who sees the trees of knowledge and understanding but misses the forest of desolation around them? Am I in denial, waiting to be angry and bargain before I accept the death of whatever is dying? Is it time to abandon the cause and fall into discouragement and despair and expiration? Is that what's troubling me?

I sweep away a layer of dust, rub my eyes, and see what's really there — a powerless little creature behind a curtain, turning wheels of fear and thunder and fire but utterly without substance, sending minions to do his bidding with the God-given abilities they always possessed and not telling them the truth until his bidding was done, his foe slaughtered — the truth that they already owned what they were looking for and didn't need a wizard in the first place.

"Save me!" the crowd shouted, and the answers they sought were already at hand, in their hearts and minds and souls, waiting to be tapped — but the smoke and mirrors confused them, and few saw through the fog, and even fewer looked behind the curtain, and only a little dog even noticed the curtain was there.

But it only took that one brave little soul to scurry over and begin to save the day. Had all this happened in one day and night lost but now found and rescued? If it only was only a day, but today and tomorrow are still full of possibilities, so stop to mourn the past, then seize the day — carpe the diem — strike for the iron is hot — but go in peace, go in peace, act in love, and peel back the curtain.

When we live despite
the urge to fear

Fear is an ugly thing. It contorts the face, boils the gut, and manifests in every unhealthy emotion – anger, worry, hatred. Fear can spread across the land, a virus more deadly than any microbe.

"Fear is the mind-killer," Frank Herbert wrote: It robs us of our reason, strips love and compassion from our hearts, and brings out the monster in us.

The children of fear are slavery, tyranny and war.

When we overcome fear, we rise.

When we rise, we turn our faces to the sun.

When we turn our faces to the sun, we begin to live. The sun nourishes, warms, gives life to the dying. Without the sun, we die in darkness.

When we live despite the urge to fear, without loathing, without anger and hatred and all of that –

when we stand instead of cowering, in other words – our spirits become invincible.

When our spirits are invincible, we have no need for the darkness.

The spirit of love is fragile and beautiful and strong and powerful all at once. It takes courage to shout love at the heart of darkness, but it's lighter, more free, an antidote for terror, and healthier for the soul.

An ounce of love is more powerful than tons of gunpowder. Love slices souls more surely than the sharpest knife. Fear is a poison; love an elixir.

I would say that I loathe fear, and I do, but loathing is a byproduct of fear and the world has enough loathing.

Better to say that in my most sane moments, I set the anger and the hatred and the anxiety aside, burying them in a place where I am free to love and to live and to laugh and to cry with joy.

Reopening and Reclaiming

Don't be scared.

No, that's not what I meant to say.

I know you're scared. I'm scared, too. It feels like everything is unraveling. People shouting at each other, wishing harm on each other, accusing each other of evil or at least evil intent. Beneath it all, the fear.

Everyone is scared, except — oh, and now I begin to sound a little paranoid — except for the ones who benefit from our fear. The sociopaths, if I'm not too harsh, who sincerely believe they know better than the huddled masses. The ones who want to rule us.

Oh, there are some people among them with a true servant attitude, people who sincerely want to protect and serve, people who believe in preserving the right to life, liberty and the pursuit of happiness and such and so.

But then there are those who — I love that the man said, "Never let a crisis go to waste," because those seven words so perfectly summarize the politics of fear.

"Never let a crisis go to waste" is an anthem of folks who want to transform society on their terms, and never mind what we want for ourselves. In their view the best time to reshape the world in accordance with their vision is when people are afraid and in chaos, so at the core they are working as hard as they can to maintain a scary and chaotic tone.

It always helps to take a breath — and another. Take as many breaths as necessary to slow your heart rate, clear your mind, and think.

Everything we do carries a risk. Yes, I could walk into a crowded room and acquire a virus that will kill me in a few days or weeks or long painful years. A deer could dash in front of my car and lead me into a fatal crash. I could go for a walk and be murdered by strangers or killed by a wild animal or a passing truck. I could sit in my home scratching out my little essays and aphorisms, in physical contact with no one, and still be overcome by an invisible germ, a fire, a burglar, a hunter's stray bullet, a fall in the shower ... Everything we do carries a risk.

Most things we worry about never happen anyway. Every moment of every day could be our last moment, but we accept that risk and carry on, even though every one of us will have a "last moment," if not this day than one day.

We step out into the world, at risk every moment, and interact with our fellow humans and with the flora and fauna and the land and the water and the air. Life is very precious, so precious that losing life is our greatest fear.

Fear can be a healthy thing, when we manage our fear and accept the risk and move forward. We need to be aware, however, that some among us want to manage our fear to manipulate us for their own purposes. "Turn your fear over to me," they coo, "and I will lead you to safety." A cage can be a very safe place if the person outside the cage feeds you and keeps you comfy.

The defining question of our age, in my opinion, is:

Do you want to be safe or free? They are not mutually exclusive, of course; you will never be completely safe or completely free. But there are those who claim relinquishing some freedom is required to ensure safety, and therein lies our conversation: How much freedom must be relinquished, and whose decision is it?

May I board a plane, for example, without guards searching me and my fellow passengers for evidence that we intend to kill everyone on board? I am willing to accept that risk, but many of those fellow passengers are not, and so I choose not to fly most of the time, out of respect for their concerns.

But it ought to be my decision, and yours, whether the risk is worth it. When someone tries to make that decision for us, *in loco parentis*, we have another kind of decision: Accept, resist, or deny.

"OK, I accept and consent to the search of my person and supposedly private property."

"OK, I understand that this is considered necessary, but I choose not to participate and will find another form of transportation."

"No, you don't have the right to decide for me, and I will attempt to board the plane myself and accept the consequences."

To be clear, I'm talking about nonviolent civil disobedience in that last example. Violence never solved anything. Centuries of "Meet the new boss, same as the old boss" have shown that violent revolution only substitutes violence for violence.

I'm talking about reclaiming control of your life. You are the boss of you. It's your life; you have to live with the choices you make; make sure those choices are actually yours.

The first step is controlling your fear. Not "Don't be scared" — Don't let being scared stop you altogether. Question why you're scared: Is someone trying to scare you, and why? Is it a rational concern that merits moving forward with caution? Are you frightened beyond reason, and if so, what's a more reasonable course of action?

But move forward. Act. Don't be paralyzed by the fear.

RECLAIMING AND RESTORING LIBERTY

What I meant to say is:

Refuse to be Afraid. Free yourself. Dream.

Restoring Liberty

"Restoring Liberty"?

How do you restore what has, in reality, never been gone?

After all, let's go back to the Declaration: "We hold these truths to be self-evident, that all men are created equal, that they are endowed by their Creator with certain unalienable Rights, that among these are Life, Liberty and the pursuit of Happiness."

Got that? "Created equal, endowed by their Creator with certain unalienable rights," that is to say, they have been yours from the moment you were created. Life, liberty, and the pursuit of happiness are "unalienable" rights, that is to say, it is a violation to infringe on these.

Be that as it may, of course, depriving people of their unalienable rights is commonplace these days, especially via government fiat, and it is necessary to reclaim these rights and restore a culture of respect for them. How do we do that?

Folks like Henry David Thoreau, Mohandas Gandhi and Martin Luther King Jr. taught a spirit of noncooperation with unjust laws. Thoreau refused to pay a poll tax to protest slavery, declaring "I cannot for an instant recognize ... as my government [that] which is the slave's government also." Gandhi led a march to the seashore to gather salt in defiance of a salt tax that imposed a jail term on anyone who dared make salt for themselves. King was jailed for leading peaceful protests against racial segregation in Birmingham, Alabama.

Restaurants and other businesses that refused to close, and even people who declined to wear a cloth mask, were publicly reviled and chastised during the pandemic even in the face of clear evidence the COVID-19 virus was going to infect its share of people no matter what the government ordered. There was negligible difference in the number of cases reported in states and nations that locked citizens down and those that allowed citizens to live their lives freely. The harder and longer government pressed, the more obvious it appeared that the orders had more to do with imposing its will than protecting health.

Even so, many would-be leaders were loathe to lift the restrictions, and they and their sycophants worked to suppress dissent from the party line to this day. But that's how you restore rights: By exercising them — speaking out, assembling peaceably, and refusing to cooperate with laws that blatantly infringe on them.

A common trait of political beasts is that once they have passed a law or tax, even a bad one, they will resist repeal with every fiber of their being. Once a right is taken away, getting it back becomes a daunting task. Close to two years after we began to reopen, some of the restrictions and government presumptions have still not been lifted, and some may be permanent, or as permanent as bad law ever can be.

It's up to us to live, be free, and pursue happiness even when — or perhaps especially when — it means defying those who would deny us those rights.

Echoes of freedom past

History doesn't repeat itself, but you can hear its echoes every day. Politicians goad each other into waging war. The actions of insane criminals are used to justify shackling the innocent. Censors in every era use the same arguments to silence original thought or dissent.

The same wind that brings echoes of past foolishness also brings echoes of lost freedoms. The hills are alive with the cries of free men and women who no longer are allowed to walk, talk or act freely. The echoes recall a time when your body was yours, what you earned was yours, your land was yours, and your honestly acquired property was yours.

Tyrants seized power or were "duly elected" on promises to protect and defend your rights to what was yours. Fool us once, shame on you. Fool us twice, shame on us. Fool us over and over, and there's too much shame to go around.

Still, I've got a bell and a song to sing, and the star of freedom never quite winks completely out. Echoes of freedom past are never quite stilled.

Short story:

'Letters from Camp'

ECHOES OF FREEDOM PAST

Introduction

When governors across the nation and even the world used a virus as an excuse to shut down the economy and place citizens under a form of house arrest in early 2020, life began to resemble the dystopian fiction that has become popular during our slow slide away from freedom. I remember walking into a popular warehouse outlet, masked, maintaining my proper distance of at least 6 feet from anyone else, and seeing widescreen TVs placed in the aisle every 20 feet or so, each tuned to a recording of Anthony Fauci reciting the CDC protocols of the day. It was like something out of *Nineteen Eighty-Four* or *Blade Runner*.

At the height of the madness, word came that Australia and other nations started to establish quarantine camps where people who tested positive for the virus were herded. Doctors and others who questioned the politicians' protocols were publicly chastised, and social media platforms suppressed and even banned alternative treatments and preventive measures. A popular meme and T-shirt urged, "Make 1984 fiction again."

It reminded me of tales of Communist China and the former Soviet Union, where we were told political dissenters or anyone who disagreed with the party line were locked away as mentally ill. My imagination began to wander to a place where political naysayers and other usual suspects were rounded up, and I spent 10 days writing blog entries from that place ...

LETTERS FROM CAMP

Day 1

Dear Bunky,

Wow, I really did not see that coming, although I guess I should have — we all should have. All those senior citizens who'd spent their lives stealing from common folk so they could establish their hippie utopia but we weren't having none of it, I guess they figured now that they were pushing 80 (and some of them plowing right past) they were running out of chances to pull the proverbial trigger.

I just never figured they'd start rounding us up for no other reason than telling them, "No, thank you, sir or ma'am," but here I am, getting off the school bus at an undisclosed location. Looks sort of like summer camp only with chain link and barbed wire between us and the woods. I have to say it's kind of pretty, although in a "WTF is this all about" sort of way.

I guess this is where I belong anyway. I mean, what did Thoreau say, "Under a government which imprisons unjustly, the true place for a just man is also a prison," right? I'd like to think I was a just man, willing and able to live and let live, and if someone has a different way of living or believing, I'm happy as a clam to leave him be if he's content to let me and mine be.

That's not how the angry old folks see it, though, nope, not a whit. The only place for dissent, in their way of looking, is behind bars or at least behind chain link. So here I am.

It doesn't seem to be too bad here, though, I mean it's like a summer camp with bunk beds, not a concentration camp. Supper was actually pretty tasty, and we had a nice conversation around the table about the weather and Sunday's game, and we were allowed to agree that the refs could have used a new prescription for their eyeglasses.

We have a lot of guest speakers who talk some rubbish about how cool the old folks' plans for the country are, and how we should study harder because we'd understand better if we would just, well, concentrate. So I guess maybe it's a concentration camp after all, huh, Bunky? LOL — I just kill me sometimes.

Anyway, there's a nice little pond here and they let us out to swim for an hour if we want between classes, and yeah, I suppose it's not too bad if you don't mind not being able to leave, although I have to admit I do kind of mind. Maybe I'll get used to it; they say you can get used to anything.

I think I'd rather be here knowing I'm a prisoner than out there thinking I'm free, you know? At least they're honest about it here.

Day 2

Dear Bunky,

After we were dismissed to our barracks and given 10 minutes to lights out, I lay in the dark and it started to sink in that this is really happening. Yesterday morning I got up from my comfy bed in our nice suburban home, and by noon we were on our way to wherever this is, encouraged at gunpoint to leave everything behind and get on the bus. If Sandi wasn't with me and depending on me not to get us killed, I probably would have resisted. Wouldn't I have?

I didn't sleep much, just kept thinking about how all this happened and when it all turned into what it's turned into. The angry old men and women who run the government were annoying with their smarmy smiles and condescending attitudes, but who really thought they were capable of this? I mean, they don't even know how to balance a checkbook, how could they possibly be able to organize camps for their enemies, if that's what they think we are? I guess I found out.

There was one guy on the bus who wouldn't stop screaming about his constitutional rights and how they can't do this and We the People ain't gonna stand for it, and one of the chaperones went back and had a couple guards hold him down while he duct-taped the guy's mouth and hands. They hustled him off the bus first when we got here. I didn't see him at supper.

If I'm angry, I'm angry at myself for getting caught flat-footed. I really didn't think guys with guns would show up at our door and haul us away, at least, not until guys with guns showed up at our door and hauled us away. I lay there in the dark afterward thinking of all the plans I could have been making, heck, we could have snuck into Canada, it's only a few hours from our house.

Breakfast this morning wasn't bad. I guess they plan to treat us humanely except for the part where they put us in a prison camp for not talking politely about our rulers. I guess I should have listened when those college kids told us to shut up and do as we're told, because it's not nice to tell the truth about the political bosses who steal from the poor to make themselves rich. I suppose they'll read this letter and you'll never get it anyway, Bunk, but I have to try. You have to be wondering why I didn't show up at work or call or anything. Come to think, why would they give me this pen and paper and tell me to write you letters? It's probably some kind of setup where they'll seize the letters and use them as proof I'm a domestic terrorist.

Well, here's my confession, Mister Judge and Ms. Jury, I think the people running the government are corrupt dopes, and they need to be gone. I should probably emphasize that by "gone" I mean arrested or at least voted out. Everyone knows I'm not violent, although I do wish I had defended myself and Sandi when I had the chance.

Right after breakfast we went back into lectures. People who believe in collective utopias sure do like to hear themselves talk. I guess I'm supposed to feel real bad about myself for believing in private property and free markets and all, because they really seem to hate that stuff and that's what landed us here. Not that what we were living with was an actual free market by any stretch.

My rear end is sore from sitting all day listening to them talk about our bright future. I think the plan is to put us back into society once we've been properly re-educated, so maybe I shouldn't be so honest telling you about how the speakers are all full of hooey. They may try harder to change my mind if I don't tone it down. If I just smile and tell them what they want to hear, maybe I'll go home sooner. Nah, it couldn't be that easy.

Day 3

Dear Bunky,

I suppose they don't want us being comforted by friends or family while we're in here. I haven't seen Sandi since we got here, and none of the people in our barracks are friends or neighbors even though I know plenty of folks who, if I belong here, have been punching their ticket to this place longer and louder than I have.

What did God create on the third day? I can't remember, and we don't get books, so I can't look it up. On the third day here, the gods of this place created boredom. Maybe it's the weekend, but the yammerers have taken the day off, no speechifying today. They just left us in the barracks and told us not to talk among ourselves, so it was lie down and sleep or think or write letters to our friends, so here I am again. I'm writing this like they're going to mail it for me and you're going to read it someday, which is probably bunk, Bunk, but you never know. Maybe the camp shrink thought this would be a peaceful way for us to let off some steam, because we're all so angry, don't you know, in their heads we're just cauldrons of hate and resentment and meanness and bigotry just waiting to explode, so rather than give us no outlet at all for our rage, they let us draw pictures and write letters to our pals. Except nobody does write anymore, right? We send texts and post on social media.

Here's something I just thought of: If anyone is a cauldron of hate and resentment and meanness and bigotry, it's the angry old women and men who have been running the show. They hate anyone who pays them no mind, they hate anyone who doesn't agree with them, they just hate all day and half the night, and then they spend the other half of the night yelling at the rest of us for being so hateful. Tossing us all into camps is their way of screaming, "Pay attention to me!" and holding their breaths and turning blue. I mean, the old figurehead popped a cork and said, "We are running out of patience with you yahoos" or some such. And when we said, "Oooh, scary, what are you going to do about it?" I guess we found out we shouldn't have baited the beast, because here we are.

The food was good for a third day in a row, though. I probably shouldn't keep saying that, because eventually they'll figure out that they can torture me by giving me crappy food or no food at all. There you go — They'll start giving me anchovie pizza every night until I start yelling "The Party is right! I need the state to take care of me! Give me that shot! Where's my electric car? Down with capitalist pigs!"

I wonder how Sandi is doing. She doesn't suffer fools very well, and this camp is run by fools.

We did get an hour outdoors today, and I walked along the water and through a path they have built through the woods. There's the usual assortment of birds, and I saw a squirrel or two — holy crap, what's going to happen to Shemp? I suppose if they were going to kill him it's already done, but I hope they gave him to a neighbor or at least a decent shelter. Everyone loves yellow labs, they'd be idiots to hurt him. Why does the idea they would hurt my dog upset me more than sticking me in this camp? He's just a dog — or maybe that's it — he's just a dog. He didn't say the old folks running the country are crooks and crazies, he just sat and loved us and did what dogs do all day and night.

I was about to write that I want to go home, but I don't think there's any going home after this, if by home you mean it's back to the life we were living before all this happened. Our eyes are opened now to the bad stuff the angry old folks were planning. I remember thinking they can't be serious about that foolishness and how would they ever enforce it? Well, yes, they are serious, and this is how they plan to pull it off. Shucks, folks, I'm speechless, they're not just old and angry pinheads, they're evil and dangerous pinheads. Should have known, I suppose.

Day 4

Dear Bunky,

Things you think about when you've been transported to a re-education camp for wrong thinking and disobeying the rulers' commands —

I wonder how life would have been different if I'd kept going after the mayor's daughter instead of falling for a girl with a free spirit and an independent mind. Don't get me wrong, I'm not blaming all this on my choices in women, I'm just wondering if I'd be a different person.

I never understood where anyone supposedly owed me anything. I always just thought since I'd been gifted this life, liberty and the pursuit of happiness, I'd better just get busy on the pursuing part of the equation, because no one was going to give me happiness on top of everything else. Even the stuff they say is free ain't free.

When my papa said no, I'm not letting you transfer to another school to follow your girlfriend, what would have happened if I'd said to hell with it, I'm following her anyway? or if I'd said, OK girl, I guess you'll have to follow me instead of the other way around?

I wonder how much of everything has to do with sex? I'm thinking that the angry old men who run the government want to push their fellow citizens around because they couldn't get a certain girl to do what they wanted, or the angry old women pass laws forcing people to turn over their hard-earned bucks because some cute guy wouldn't give them what they wanted? Do you know what I mean, Sigmund, I mean, Bunky?

Why do we give a flaming flamingo about who's in first place and how many games behind is the home team?

Why do we spend so much time wondering "What if I'd done things differently way back when?" instead of "What if I try this next?"

I wonder why it feels like the end of it all when you're tossed in a re-education camp. I suppose it IS the end of the old life and we're all getting fitted for the new normal. Am I allowed to use that phrase, or is "the new normal" a brand for free people? And by free people I mean the folks who are still out there and moving around. I wasn't seeing many free people the last time I was out there, which seems a long time ago now even if it was less than a week.

I started this letter thinking about how life would have been different if I'd made different choices back in high school, but I wonder how life would have been different if I'd made other choices last year or even last week. What if I had said "no" when they told me everyone was going to have to stay home, and what if I had said "yes" or at least "OK" when they said get in line and submit last week when I said "Let me think about it" because I was thinking "Nope, no way, no how." Part of me figures this has been coming a long time, and part of me figures they're making this up as they go. I want to believe they just came up with this idea, but on the other hand they built this camp and got it all safe, sound and secure before the campers were moved in, which takes a lot more planning than "We are running out of patience and we're going to have to figure out what to do about that." This sure doesn't feel very spur-of-the-moment, but what do I know?

I don't think there's an alternate universe where I made different choices and an alternate me is living happily ever after in the mansion with the mayor's daughter. I think this camp is the singular sum total that came out when I added up my choices. If this is my final destination, I'm disappointed, but it was one hell of a ride to get here, wasn't it?

And I gotta say again, they do feed us well. Hey, Bunky, maybe the angry old men and women are cannibals from outer space and "To Serve Man" is a recipe book after all. It kind of all makes sense if you see it that way.

Day 5

Dear Bunky,

I got to see Sandi today. She looked great except for the part where she was a wreck — exhausted looking, hair all disheveled, and acting as beaten as I've ever seen her. She was real depressed and didn't feel like talking.

It kind of shook me to see her like that. I mean, I

know how she feels, I look at our immediate prospects and all I see is chain link fence and barbed wire — some of the most beautiful nature I've ever seen on the other side, but we're prisoners here. We grew up in the land of the free and political camps were something other countries did — bad countries with evil regimes — well, except for if you were Japanese Americans in World War II, and that was a long, long time ago and we feel bad about it now, don't we?

But this is today, and if you told me last week that this is where we were headed, rounding up people who spoke out against The Powers That Be, I would have said come on, man, we're being ruled by a bunch of angry old men and women like the Soviets in the '80s when one tired eighty-something communist dies in office and is replaced by a guy almost as old or older, but it's not like they're setting up gulags or anything. And heck, a week later and I'm on Day 5 in a gulag. And Sandi looks and acts like her whole world died. I guess I feel that way, too, but I'm better at keeping up appearances.

The only thing good about the whole place is the food. Pork chops cooked to perfection tonight, apple sauce on the side, potatoes and green beans, and pumpkin pie for dessert.

And a whole day listening to people talking about how much better the country will be when we are release some day. They'll have their great social safety net programs all installed and taking care of us by then. We won't have to worry if we get sick or nothing.

I hate to cut it short, Bunky, but I gotta admit I don't feel like writing much more, and we probably have to go listen to another lecture soon.

See you around, someday.

Day 6

Dear Bunky,

How does this happen? Another remarkable meal from the camp chef. Remember the beef Strogonoff we had at that diner in Northport? This almost as good.

Every day here is pretty much the same. A few

hours in class being taught the glories of the Party and its plans to take care of everything, a little exercise, and decent meals. For prisoners, we're treated better than you might expect.

Let me give you an example — one guy just ups and starts screaming in the middle of our walk today, you know, can't take it anymore, this is supposed to be America, that sort of thing. In the movies, he'd probably get manhandled and beaten, you know, the old "Silence! I keel you!" but one of the docs just walked over, put an arm around his shoulder, and walked him away.

Please don't think I'm suddenly OK with being taken from home and dropped into a Soviet-style re-education camp. I'm just adjusting to the fact that this is what The Powers That Be see as necessary to maintain order for the common good. They're not evil, we just disagree. Maybe we'd do the same if the roles were reversed.

Usually this is where you probably start worrying about me, I suppose. Or maybe you've been worrying all along. I appreciate that, but really, I'm OK. I'm your same old buddy, just ruminating a little.

So that's the news from Lake Wherever-This-Is. Same old, same old, right down the line.

Day 7

Dear Sergeant,

For the record, this is the apology letter you demanded after you read my last letter to my friend Bunky. I guess I understand why you were unhappy and wouldn't let me write him today.

Until now, I have to admit, I thought the staff of this camp were stupid thugs. But you were bright enough to realize I left a short message to Bunky in the first letter of each paragraph yesterday.

Catastrophe will not descend on the camp if my pal realizes that while describing camp life in reassuring tones, I was also spelling out a plea for him to "HELP US." It's not like Bunky could help even if he wanted to, he doesn't know where I am. Neither do I, for that matter.

Kudos, however, for finding my other implanted message. You have to know Bunky and me pretty well to suss out that both of us vomited after eating the beef Strogonoff at the Northport Diner. My cover is blown, I can't say nice things about the food here anymore. Damn.

Yesterday I guess I was more frustrated than I realized about being here. I know you guys are only following orders, so I do owe you an apology, and I hope you'll accept it.

On the other hand, I don't have any kind words for the angry men and women who have seized control of the government and enabled this Soviet-style camp for American citizens. I don't want to get you in trouble, but I can't believe you take those people seriously.

Under our system, or least the system I grown up in, people were allowed to criticize or even make fun of our leaders, to disagree with a law or a lawmaker, and to move about the country freely. Leaders who are confident in their beliefs ought not fear exposure to lesser ideas.

Yet these doddering old fools drove this country toward dictatorship for years, and now they're tossing wrong-thinkers like me into camps surrounded by chain link and barbed wire.

Obviously they're not very confident their ideology will fly with the masses. They have to know you can't win a philosophical battle by throwing dissenters into a cage, but here I am with a few hundred of my fellow travelers.

Usurping a 200-year republic without an open revolution seems impossible, but here we are, happily living a Soviet lifestyle with empty shelves in grocery stores, thought police on every corner, rampant Pravda-style journalism, and citizens snickering at the doddering old fools in charge even as they cower and obey the rules.

Can you imagine the heyday historians will have years from now as they dissect the fall of the American

Empire? It happened in a blink of an eye. It happened tortuously slowly over decades.

Other campers here aren't taking it as calmly as I am. Even I'm not sure why I'm calm about it. Intellectually I'm outraged, but I can't bring myself to feel any rage. Maybe I'm still in shock.

Much has been made over the old adage that it's not the votes that count as much as who counts the votes. Part of bringing down the republic was destroying everyone's faith in the election process. For years one party screamed about rigged elections, then they won a couple and now the other party is screaming.

Me, I have no use for either party. I suppose if the other party opened some camps, I'd be tossed into theirs. That's another reason I don't take this personally, Sarge.

"I got no need to beat you, I just want to go my way." One of my favorite Malcolm Reynolds quotes, and that's my philosophy, too. I have no beef with people I disagree with, as long as we leave each other alone.

Everyone agrees with that approach. Or at least I thought so.

For what it's worth, I'm sorry I've been less than a model camper. I'm doing my best to do what I'm told, but I just can't manage to think what you tell me to think.

Undulating thoughts just keep bubbling up about freedom and liberty and resisting tyrants with every breath.

Can you accept my apology even if it's half-hearted? I'm sort of trying here.

Know this: My days of leaving secret messages at the margins are done. I hope you'll let me write my letter to Bunky tomorrow.

Day 8

Dear Bunky,

I don't think the people here have any sense of humor. I wrote an apology letter to the sergeant in charge of these barracks, but I included a little message in disguise for him and holy moley was he not a happy camper when he found it. I suppose I was a little rude, but I was sent to bed without any supper, and you know how much I look forward to meals here.

It's starting to feel like fall around here, and the leaves are turning nice shades of red and yellow and orange. Well, there's one clue about where they took us — closer to Maine than to Louisiana. At this rate you'll find me in 20 years or so.

I have a funny feeling I've seen my last snowfall, though. I mean, they hauled us off to this re-education camp to wash our brains clean of these funny notions we have about freedom and individual rights, and here I am still thumbing my nose and not getting with the program.

I'm not seeing prospects for a happy ending. Do they still teach Patrick Henry in schools anymore? Somehow I doubt it. I know how he must have felt when he said give me liberty or, well, you know ...

Day 9

Dear Mr. Buncio:

Thank you for your service as designated recipient of mail from People's Prisoner LPX-1139. Acting as a sounding board is a sometimes difficult but often therapeutic role for our mentally ill clients.

I regret to inform you that your service is complete, as your friend is deceased. He developed symptoms two days ago and went downhill very quickly. I am sorry for your loss — I know that is a common thing to say and can sound insincere, but as the supervisor of his barracks I get to know everyone personally and it truly hurts to lose a client, especially when they are showing progress as your friend was.

Facilities like ours perform a necessary service in these troubled times when misinformation and dangerous ideas are spread like a deadly virus among the people. Support from friends like yourself is an invaluable aid in the recovery process. We all were encouraged by LPX-1139's progress and confident he would have soon been healthy enough for a full reinsertion into civilized society.

A modest compensation will be placed in your digital account as our thanks for being such a valuable advocate for your friend in these challenging times.

Yours very sincerely,

Day 10

Dear Bunky,

I bet you never expected to see this handwriting ever again, huh? Well, I don't know what BS they told you — probably that I'm dead, right? — but here's the real deal.

I'm out. They're not as smart as they think they are. A couple of the guys figured out how to get past the security system. I can't tell you more in case this letter ever finds its way into their hands. Not that you would do that, Bunk, but they know we're pals and they will probably want your opinion about stuff and maybe take a look around your place. You can decide to self-destruct this letter or keep it safe for whatever purpose.

Sandi's dead. Really. I'm still trying to process that.

They told me she caught the bug and went down quickly, but I think she either killed herself or got herself killed somehow. They use the bug to cover any mysterious happenings. Remember the guys I told you about who freaked out on the bus coming over and in the mess hall? I asked the sarge about them, and you know what he said? Yep, the bug got 'em. Hell, it can be an awful disease, so it's good cover for any shenanigans.

I don't know how I feel about losing her. Remember how calm I was about getting snatched and I thought maybe I was in shock? It's like that. She was really down the one time they let me see her, but she always had this fierce love of life. I can see where this place could take that away from her, but it would make more sense if I heard she pissed off a guard and got, you know, the ultimate punishment. That just sounds more like the Sandi I knew.

The people I'm with have a few ideas about getting the camp liberated and closed. Of course, after we got out we figured out where we are, and sorry, Bunk, I can't share any more than that. Just know that all is not lost.

How did it come to this, that a bunch of angry old people could wave some toys and candy at us and we followed like little kids sucked in by a perv? It's so obvious how angry and manipulative they are, but so many people only see the bright shiny objects. I guess you really can fool some people all the time.

But not everyone.

It's been great knowing you, Bunky. I know you had to give my letters back to the sergeant every day as part of my "therapy," but they don't know about this letter. I'd appreciate it if it stayed that way, but I know you have to protect yourself, too — so do what you think is right.

You probably won't hear from me again unless we both arrive safely on the other side of whatever you want to call this. Good luck, God bless, have fun, whatever. Just don't let the bastards get you down.

Postscript

The short story "Letters from Camp" began as 10 blog posts that emerged from some thoughts I had while reading the late L. Neil Smith's wonderful collection of writings on liberty, *Lever Action*. I imagined a series of letters from a re-education gulag after the eventual triumph of the folks who want to "transform" our way of life.

Specifically, the series grew from a comment Smith made in 2000 about the then-leaders of China:

"...it's worrisome to deal with a handful of geriatric bastards who know they won't have to live with the consequences of plunging their nation into total war."

I started musing that perhaps we should consider the motivations of the seventysomething and eightysomething tyrants who are running the U.S. ship of state into the ground — the senile and not-so-senile so-called leaders who cling to power with the fervor they once accused their adversaries of clinging to guns and religion — the basket of deplorables who seek to reshape America into a collective utopia and to hell with individual rights.

Is it so hard to imagine they could dispense with "cancel culture" and simply round up the wrong-thinkers?

Are they callous enough to aim the ship of state into the rocks knowing that, like the Chinese Communist leaders of 2000, they won't have to live with the consequences? Is this administration the final act of a generation of collectivists who would rather leave chaos behind than a free and open society?

The Old Guard who ran China then and the Old Guard who run the United Soviet States of America now have much in common. They believe they can run the lives of millions upon millions better than those individuals can rule themselves. Or wait, do they even care about those people in the first place, as long as they are the ones lording over the rest of us? There has always been a distinct air of "Do as I say, not as I do" about them, because they consider themselves above the scrutiny of whom they consider lesser human beings.

They have become wealthy on tax dollars and sit in their mansions or fly around the world burning the fossil fuel they would deny the next generation, calling US deplorable and making assumptions about "the common folk."

Also by Warren Bluhm

Refuse to be Afraid (2010, 2020)

Fear has become the motivating factor in this contemporary world of ours. Life is portrayed as a maelstrom of forces beyond the power of the individual to tame.

It's a lie. You can tame the maelstrom, if you can tame your fear.

This short but powerful book is designed to help you plow through the nagging doubts and outright fears of various sizes and shapes that are keeping you from living your best life. Faced with a scary reality, it challenges you to navigate past the anxiety, refuse to be afraid, and free yourself to move on to your dreams.

The book has been expanded and revised over the years, but the original edit of the 2010 classic retains its punch. Fight the Fear!

"When this wonderful little book by Warren Bluhm first dropped into my hands a decade ago, I thought it was important. Today, I think it's particularly vital." — Wally Conger

Choose the original edit or 10th Anniversary Edition.

How to Play a Blue Guitar (2020)

The Zero Aggression Principle states, "No one has the right, under any circumstances, to initiate force against another human being for any reason whatever; nor should anyone advocate the initiation of force, or delegate it to anyone else."

This quirky little book contains two dozen poems, short stories, prose poems and aphorisms around the theme of finding a way to live and let live in peace — to co-exist without forcing a way of life on people.

Because "The way you play a blue guitar is the same as the way you play any guitar ... It's built with the same workings, potential melodies and chords, hopes and dreams as any other color guitar. Kind of like people."

FULL: Rockets, Bells & Poetry (2021)

"My God, I'm full of words."

"The dance of the pen across the page is a deer prancing in the snow, kids racing through the grass, a performance car zipping across the flats so fast the videographer struggles to keep the machine in the frame."

Here are notes, aphorisms and poems in three mini-collections: "The Creative Soul," reflections on making art and the power of words; "Live Free Or Die," thoughts about liberty, self-expression and emerging from dystopia; and "You Can Do This," encouraging words of finding light in a darkening world.

24 flashes (2021)

If you only have a minute, this book is for you. This little book contains 24 very short stories, most of them fewer than 1,000 words, which fits many people's definition of flash fiction; hence the title. You'll find fantasy, romance, science fiction, horror, suspense, maybe even a thriller, all in the time it takes to read this blurb. Buy it now. You've got the time.

Gladness is Infectious (2020)

Add to the beauty or add to the despair: Each of us has two choices every day.

The choice is there, every morning – to ride the light out of darkness and live in peace, striving for harmony against the discord.

A Bridge at Crossroads: 101 Encouragements (2019)

Life is better lived when you search for the light and not the dark. Here are 101 encouragements for when you're about to embark on a new adventure, when you're wrestling with doubt, when you could use a gentle push, or all of the above.

Myke Phoenix: The Complete Novelettes (2019)

From the pulse-pounding origin story to the fateful attack from beyond space and history that changed Astor City forever, it's all here. For the first time ever, you can have all 16 novelettes and two short stories in the Myke Phoenix canon collected in one edition. Here is the entire saga from the moment a mysterious spirit living in an unusual piece of pottery selects Paul Phillips, to the final showdown with the megalomaniacal talking dinosaur Deinonychus, with a new introduction by the author.

The Imaginary Revolution (2012)

The people of Sirius 4 tried to overcome tyranny the old-fashioned way: by force. It turned out to be an imaginary revolution, replacing one violent regime with another. Raymond Douglas Kaliber suggested another way: that free people living by a spirit of non-aggression could live in peace and prosperity with one another. Before he could launch that bold experiment, however, he had to defeat the greatest tyrant of them all: his best friend ... Set in the same universe as the interplanetary romp The Imaginary Bomb, this novel sets a different tone, told in the voice of the man who led a planet to true freedom.

A Scream of Consciousness (2011)

There has to be something more to life than moving through a haze. And every now and then, it gets to you. You just want to wake up, smile at God and the universe and shout: I'm alive! I'm here! I'm ready to make a difference! That's a scream of consciousness. This book is about getting conscious and staying alive, moment by moment.

The Imaginary Bomb (2008)

So his ex is a terrorist. Now what?

It's bad enough that government couriers have commandeered Bob's space freighter to transport a secret cargo.

Now his ship has been hijacked again by polite thugs led by a masked woman whose voice sounds awfully familiar. She and her gang take the secret cargo.

The couriers say it's a gang of thieves. But the government took his ship, so who are the thieves?

Bob has to figure out which side he's on before something else goes horribly wrong, like the moon exploding. Wait, what?

You'll love The Imaginary Bomb because everybody enjoys a fast-paced space opera with a love triangle.

Edited by Warren Bluhm

Resistance to Civil Government:
On the Duty of Civil Disobedience
Henry David Thoreau
Letters to the Citizens of the United States
Thomas Paine
A Little Volume of Secrets
As A Man Thinketh, Acres of Diamonds, The Science of Getting Rich

THE ROGER MIFFLIN COLLECTION

The Haunted Bookshop
Christopher Morley
Men in War
Andreas Latzko
Trivia
Logan Pearsall Smith
The Man Who Was Thursday
G.K. Chesterton
The Demi-Gods
James Stephens
The Story of My Heart
Richard Jefferies
Note-Books
Samuel Butler